Elon Musk

What YOU Can Learn from His AMAZING Life

By

Biographies For Kids

implied. Readers acknowledge that the author is not engaging in the rendering of legal, financial, medical or professional advice.

By reading this document, the reader agrees that under no circumstances are we responsible for any losses, direct or indirect, which are incurred as a result of the use of information contained within this document, including, but not limited to, —errors, omissions, or inaccuracies.

Table Of Contents

Elon's Childhood

Elon Reeve Musk was born in Pretoria, Transvaal, South Africa, on June 28, 1971. His father, Errol Musk, was an electromechanical engineer, sailor and pilot. His mother, Maye Musk, was a model and dietician. Elon also had a younger brother, Kimbal, and a younger sister, Tosca, growing up.

As a child Elon was what you would call an "introvert." What exactly is an "introvert?" Well, it's the opposite of an "extrovert." But what does that mean? Well, most psychologists (people who study things like this) would tell you that two thirds of all the people you meet are extroverts. They get energized being around other people, laughing and talking about just about anything. Nothing wrong with that!

An introvert, on the other hand, likes people too. However, unlike the outgoing extrovert they only have a limited supply of energy they can share. Being around people actually drains them of energy and can make them feel tired and worn out. This is why introverts typically make only a few close friends and value their alone time. If they have to be around a big group of people, introverts like Elon typically need some downtime to recharge. Some people think introverts are shy but that's often not the case. They love to think and share ideas about big things. If you are a friend with an introvert you should be very proud! Introverts don't make friends with just anyone. If they've made friends with you it means they think you're special in some way. At any rate it doesn't matter whether you're an introvert or an extravert. The world needs both to go around.

Elon's parents were divorced in 1980 and as a result young Elon and his siblings were mainly raised by their father. Despite the divorce the family was still quite well off and Errol was able to take them on trips to Europe, Hong Kong, and the United States. However, although the family didn't lack for money Errol still insisted that his children do their own chores and learn how to cook. Do you like doing chores? Most kids don't, but as a member of a family you have a responsibility to pitch in. You may not like it now but doing chores can help you develop a work ethic that will help you later in life. It certainly helped Elon, as we shall soon see.

"I guess I was a bit of an autocratic father – 'do this, do that'. I was a single parent, and they simply had to help out." – Errol Musk on raising his children.

What was Elon like as a kid? Well, like I said before, young Elon was an introvert who loved to learn and think. He read everything he could get his hands on. This is very important as the more you KNOW, the more you can DO. This is a habit that Elon has kept up into his adult life. He is a lifelong learner, and nothing makes Elon happier than learning something new!

"I would see him frequently in or around the library. Musk had an above-average interest in

matters outside the normal curriculum, and the library – these were pre-internet years – was the place to gain further knowledge" – Ewyn van den Aardweg, Elon's former geography teacher, on his learning habits.

One of the things that young Elon loved to learn about was computers. His family owned a Commodore Vic-20, a Spectra Video and an IBM. The personal computers Elon had were very different to the computers we have today! There was no Internet to connect to, the computers didn't use a mouse and they couldn't even talk to one another! Nonetheless, to Elon they were magical and he quickly taught himself how to program using a programming language called BASIC. He even programmed a video game himself and named it BLASTAR! Although the game was VERY simple it did work and Elon was able to sell it to a computer magazine for $500. That was a lot of money in those days! If you want to play BLASTAR! yourself you can find it here:

http://blastar-1984.appspot.com/

"[It was] a trivial game ... but better than Flappy Bird" – Elon Musk commenting on the game he designed as a child.

WHEN ELON WAS YOUNG HE TAUGHT HIMSELF HOW TO PROGRAM AND EVEN WROTE HIS OWN GAME.

Growing up was not easy for Elon. Although he was REALLY smart he was also socially awkward. He was just different from everyone else and as a result he attracted the attention of bullies. Why do bullies bully? Typically, it's because they lack empathy for other people or

9

because they feel bad about themselves. In order to make themselves feel better they attack others and run them down. They don't understand that it's always better for everyone to build others up! Here's a little trick for you. If you are ever feeling bad or sad don't lash out at other people. Instead, find someone and either offer to help them or offer them a compliment. It can be as simple as, "That's a very pretty dress you're wearing" or "Can I help you cross the street?" It's a law of nature that what you put out into the world you will get back three-fold. When you make others feel happy and positive, pretty soon you'll start to feel better too! This is much better than making others feel bad and, in the end, making others feel bad doesn't help you much either. Unfortunately, most bullies do not understand this.

At any rate Elon was bullied horribly as a child. One time he was pushed down a stairwell and beaten so badly that he had to be taken to a hospital. In fact, he was hurt so badly that later as an adult he had to have an operation to clear one of his nostrils. If this sounds terrible that's because it is. Sadly, back then we didn't have the awareness of bullying that we have today and Elon simply endured it without telling anyone. You, however, don't have to do this. If you are being bullied, share what is happening to you with your parents or another trusted adult like a teacher. You can also check the back of this book for some advice on how to avoid being bullied and what to do if you are. Always remember, however, that if you are bullied it ISN'T YOUR FAULT, just like it wasn't Elon's fault. You're not the only person who has experienced this. Just like Elon, you are stronger than you know and you WILL GET THROUGH IT!

"For some reason they decided that I was it, and they were going to go after me nonstop. That's what made growing up difficult" – Elon Musk on being bullied as a child.

Elon's College Career

In 1989, Elon Musk turned seventeen and decided to attend school in Canada along with his brother Kimbal. The school he initially chose was the Queen's School of Business in Kingston, Ontario. Remember how I mentioned before that doing chores helped to install a strong work ethic in Elon? This is where it really started to shine. At college, he was constantly working and studying everything he could.

"It's rare to have the mix of business knowledge with the understanding of physics and science, along with the raw intelligence and focus. He's always known what he wanted to do." – Elon's college friend Dominic Thompson.

I think you can see what makes Elon so special and learning from his example perhaps can help you be special too. By having a wide variety of interests Elon Musk was able to develop a very unique *talent stack*. What is a talent stack? Well, it's simply some things you may be good at. Any individual talent you possess may not be that unique. However, what you will find is that really successful people often combine their talents in unique ways to achieve amazing results. For example, Elon Musk is a great businessman. Being a businessman requires a certain set of skills like hiring people, accounting, advertising and planning. If these were his only skills he could have found a job as a businessman in just about any company in America. However, Elon was also really interested in physics and science, not to mention science fiction. If that were his only skillset he would be primed to be a scientist of some kind. However, combine these two different skill sets and you are able to create a unique company like Space X. See what I mean?

What individual skills and talents do you have? Everyone is good at something. Never be afraid to experiment and try new things. Also, always be on the lookout for ways to combine your skills in unique ways. You may not create the next Space X, but I bet you can create something unique and wonderful!

"When Elon gets into something, he develops just this different level of interest in it than other people. That is what differentiates Elon from the rest of humanity." – Navaid Farooq, Elon's college roommate.

When Elon was at college he didn't have very much money. He therefore had to try to make extra cash whenever he could. One thing he did for money was building and servicing computers for people. Remember how young Elon loved computers when he was growing up? Once again, on a much smaller scale, he was able to combine this skill with his business sense to make some extra money.

"I could build something to suit their needs like a tricked-out gaming machine or a simple word processor that cost less than what they could get in a store. Or if their computer didn't boot properly or had a virus, I'd fix it. I could pretty

much solve any problem." – Elon Musk on his
dorm-based computer business.

Are you beginning to see how powerful talent stacks can be?

Selling and servicing computers was a good side business for Elon when he was actually in school. However, during school breaks he had to find other ways to make money. One of the jobs Elon did was cleaning out the boiler room of a lumber mill for $18 an hour. This was a really hard job, but Elon was a hard worker. In order to do it you had to put on what is known as a Hazmat suit. A Hazmat suit covers your entire body and is meant to protect you from hazardous materials. Elon needed this because inside the boilers he had to clean were often steaming hot toxic materials. Definitely not a fun job, but Elon did it anyway!

"Someone else on the other side has to shovel it (toxic materials) into a wheelbarrow. If you stay in there for more than thirty minutes, you get too hot and die." – Elon Musk on the difficulties of cleaning out a boiler.

After two years at the Queen's School of Business, Elon transferred to the University of Pennsylvania on a scholarship. He loved it there and he proved to be a very competitive person. He loved to compare his test scores to those of others and he enjoyed participating in public speaking competitions. What he really enjoyed about it, however, was that he was able to make some really good friends with like-minded people. There's a lesson for you here too. Remember how young Elon was bullied? Can you imagine how he must have felt? What do you think 20-year-old Elon would have told his younger self? I suspect it would have been something like, "I know it's tough, but hang in there, buddy. Better times are just around the corner. Wait until you meet the friends you're going to have!"

"There were some nerds there. He so enjoyed them. I remember going for lunch with them, and they were talking physics things... They would laugh out loud. It was cool to see him so happy." – Elon's mother, Maye Musk, on the changes she observed in her son when he was attending university.

One of the friends he made at the University of Pennsylvania was a young man named Adeo Ressi. Together, they rented a ten-bedroomed home that they converted into a fraternity house. In case you don't know, a "fraternity" is basically like a club in which people with shared interests share a space and often have fun. In this case, Elon and Adeo made a club for all of their nerdy friends. What's more, on the weekend they would often convert their fraternity into a nightclub and charge admission. (Can you see the "talent stack" at work once again?) Sometimes, up to five hundred people would show up! Although Elon liked to meet people, he was not a big drinker or partier. He could often be seen walking around the parties with a single Diet Coke in his hand.

"... somebody had to stay sober during these parties. I was paying my own way through college and could make an entire month's rent in one night. Adeo was in charge ... around the house, and I would run the party." – Elon Musk on how he managed the parties he threw.

To his friend, Adeo Ressi, Elon was *"...the most straight-laced dude"* he'd ever met. *"He never drank. He never did anything. Zero. Literally nothing."* I think from this we can see that Elon Musk was never a big partier, but that's OK. He knew who he was and what he wanted to do, and it didn't involve getting drunk at parties.

Elon Begins His Career in Business

As Elon's time at the University of Pennsylvania began to come to an end he started to consider what his next move would be. He still really liked video games and briefly considered becoming a video game designer. However, deep down he really wanted to pursue projects that would have positive impacts on the world. Although video games can bring a lot of joy, they are not really world changing. He wanted to do more than simply design video games.

"I really like computer games, but then if I made really great computer games, how much effect would that have on the world? It wouldn't have a big effect." – Elon Musk on his decision NOT to pursue video games as a career.

Another thing that Elon was sure about was that he wanted to create things. Being an investor in some capacity, for example, held no interest for him. He wanted to get his hands dirty and create products or services that would help people.

"I like to make technologies real that I think are important for the future and useful in some sort of way." – Elon Musk on why merely being an investor was not for him.

After thinking about it for a while Elon decided that his passions were in areas such as the Internet (which was just getting started at the time), space travel and renewable energy. In college he had actually written a paper on solar energy entitled, *"The Importance of Being Solar."* He even drew up plans for future power stations that would use giant Earth-orbiting reflectors to focus sunlight on energy collectors on the ground. He was always passionate about space travel and helping man to become an "interplanetary species" (his words) would certainly have a big impact. The Internet as we know it was just beginning and he thought that there must be opportunities there. The possibilities in all three of these areas were potentially enormous. The question was, where to start?

Initially, Elon Musk decided to go to Stanford University in order to get his PhD in energy physics. This would likely be useful if he wanted to do something with solar power in the future, not to mention rocketry. However, as I've said, the Internet was just beginning to take off and Elon found himself constantly thinking about it. Sometimes ideas are like that. They just stick around in your head, almost nagging you. Ideas like this should be taken seriously, and Elon realized he needed to act on this Internet idea. He decided to defer his graduate studies at Stanford in order to do something on the Internet side of things.

The first thing he did was to apply for a job at a company called Netscape. It's hard to imagine now, but at that time the idea of surfing the Internet with a browser was a completely new concept and Netscape had the best browser on the market. Netscape was THE hot company and

Elon thought it would be really cool to work for them. He actually wrote to them, enquiring about possible employment, but they never wrote back. Elon thought he understood why- his degrees were in economics and physics, and not computer science. Nonetheless, he knew that he was still really good with computers so he actually went down to the Netscape offices in the hopes of getting a job. However, once he got there he was too shy to talk to anyone! After hanging around for a bit and not talking to a living soul, Elon left and decided to start his own Internet company.

ELON WANTED TO WORK AT NETSCAPE, BUT WAS TOO SHY TO ASK FOR AN INTERVIEW!

I think there are a few lessons we can take from this. One of them is that we should never judge a book by its cover. When Netscape received Elon Musk's letter they likely dismissed the idea of employing him due to his inappropriate degrees. If they had TALKED to him, however, they might have realized just how brilliant he was! Netscape doesn't really exist today as a company. (It ceased support for its browser back in 2008.) How might history have been different if they'd given a young Elon Musk a chance? The other lesson here is that everyone can lack confidence and be a little shy from time to time. If this is how you are sometimes then don't let it bother you. Always remember that the great Elon Musk couldn't talk his way into an interview at Netscape! Also remember that when one door closes, another one opens. For Elon, the closed door was Netscape. But the closing of this door allowed him to walk through the open door of what was to become his first Internet company.

The first Internet company that Elon started was called Zip2. The original founders of the company were himself, his brother Kimbal, and a friend named Greg Kouri. They founded the company in Palo Alto, California, using $28,000 from Elon's dad and $6000 from Kouri. Zip2 used the power of the Internet to create online city guides that newspapers could use to connect their advertisers with customers. It proved to be a very popular service to the point that Compaq, a computer company, bought it in February, 1999, for 307 million dollars. As a founder, Elon earned 22 million dollars from the sale.

With 22 million dollars in the bank a lot of people might have retired right there, but Elon Musk is not most people. The very next month he used 10 million dollars of his own money to found a new Internet company called X.com. Elon had dreams of X.com becoming a virtual, online bank that could facilitate money transfers over the Internet. The following year, Elon oversaw the merger of X.com with another company named Confinity, which you have probably never heard of. However, Confinity itself had a working online money transfer service they called PayPal, which you probably have heard of. The newly merged company focused on the PayPal business as it showed the most growth, and eventually the entire company was renamed PayPal in 2001. By that point Elon, however, had already been removed from the company as its CEO by its board of directors. The reason for this was that Elon had wanted to move the company's computer infrastructure from UNIX machines to Windows. The board hadn't agreed with this plan so they had removed him as CEO. Elon remained with the board and kept his 11% of the company stock, which turned out to be a good move. This is because the online auction site eBay decided to buy PayPal in 2002 for 1.5 billion dollars in stock. From this deal Elon earned 165 million dollars.

ELON, PICTURED HERE WITH PETER THIEL, EARNED MORE THAN 165 MILLION DOLLARS WHEN PAYPAL WAS SOLD TO EBAY.

Once again, with 165 million dollars in the bank you might think that Elon would retire and take it easy. Taking it easy, however, is not a part of Elon Musk's personality. After university he had decided that he wanted to spend his life doing big things in the areas of the Internet (mission accomplished), renewable energy and space exploration. With his newly earned riches he decided it was time to do something with space.

Space X

Initially, Elon wanted to use existing rockets to land miniature greenhouses on the planet Mars. He called his idea the "Mars Oasis" project and it was meant to be the first step in establishing a human colony on Mars. Whatever you want to say about Elon Musk, he certainly doesn't lack ambition! The existing rockets he had in mind were refurbished intercontinental ballistic missiles (ICBMs) that he thought he could acquire from Russia. Elon decided to take a trip there to see if this was a possibility.

ELON'S LONG TERM DREAM IS TO COLONIZE MARS.

Elon travelled to Russia with his college buddies Adeo Ressi and Jim Cantrell, who had worked in the aerospace equipment supply business. Adeo thought Elon was crazy to get into the rocket business and repeatedly told him so. He made a video of rockets blowing up on launch one after the other and showed them to Elon. He even made jokes to Elon that went something like this:

Adeo to Elon – "Hey, Elon, want to know how to make a small fortune in the rocket business?"

Elon Musk – "You bet, how do I do it?"

Adeo – "Easy. In order to make a small fortune in the rocket business you just need to start with a big one!"

The fact of the matter is that there was a lot of truth in what Adeo was telling Elon. The rocket business was VERY risky and launching rockets is a very tricky business. Elon took Adeo's criticisms very seriously and even appreciated them. One of Elon Musk's driving philosophies is that he greatly values criticism and failure, as without them you cannot change and grow. This is another lesson you can learn from Elon Musk. Constructive criticism can make you better and nothing teaches harder and more valuable lessons than failure. Don't avoid criticism or failure. Embrace them. See them as positive things. They will make you stronger in the long run.

Elon and his friends met several people involved in the Russian rocket industry. However, none of them took Elon and his ideas seriously. They thought he was an amateur and a dreamer who had no idea of what he was talking about. In fact, they thought so little of Elon and had such contempt for him and his friends that one of them even spat on them!

"One of their chief designers spit on me and Elon because he thought we were full of s**t" – Jim Cantrell, recalling their less than successful meetings with the Russians.

Once again, although they didn't have to be so rude about it, the Russians DID have a point. What Elon was planning WAS outrageous. However, this is the role that entrepreneurs and businessman can play in a society. They are constantly on the lookout for new ways to do and produce things that others may want. Everyone had thought that Henry Ford was crazy when he wanted to produce a car for the masses, but he had done it anyway with the Model T. Everyone thought that Steve Jobs was crazy when he wanted to create a computer that everyone could use. The Apple II showed it could be done. Do you see the pattern here and how it relates to talent stacks? Engineers who only have engineering talents can often only work on things that are right in front of them. It takes the talents of imagination and vision that great entrepreneurs possess to really create revolutionary things. This is the talent stack that Elon Musk possessed and the spitting Russian rocket designers did not.

As he and his friends travelled back to America, Elon started to think about building his own rockets. He did some rough calculations and decided he could build and launch rockets at three percent of the cost of using the Russian ones. Remember how I told you that when one door closes another, and often much better one, opens? This is a prime example of this phenomenon. The door to using Russian rockets had slammed in Elon's face, but the door to the founding of Space X had just opened.

THE FALCON HEAVY, READY FOR LAUNCH.

Elon Musk founded the Space Exploration Technologies Corporation, or Space X, in May 2002. Now, when you found a company with the lofty goals that Space X has (turning mankind into a multi-planet species is certainly lofty) your first step is to find the best people to work for you. The first person Elon hired was a well-regarded rocket engineer and designer named Tom Mueller. At that time Tom was doing work for an aerospace company called TRW and had already designed a rocket engine for them. In his spare time, he and other like-minded individuals enjoyed building rockets and launching them in the desert. Through talking to other rocket scientists, Elon heard about Tom and decided he had to meet him. At Tom's house he was shown a homemade rocket that Tom was building and Elon was impressed. His only question for Tom was, "Can you build something bigger?" With the resources that Elon was gathering at Space X Tom certainly could build a bigger rocket engine. Elon hired him on the spot.

The first rocket that Space X designed and launched was named the Falcon 1. Elon named it after the Millennium Falcon from *Star Wars* and it used a single Merlin rocket engine that Tom designed. The first THREE times the Falcon 1 was launched all ended in failure. Many people in the press, as well as Space X investors, were becoming increasingly skeptical of Elon and the Space X team. Despite the doubters, however, Space X kept working towards their goal and the fourth launch of the Falcon 1 was a huge success. Based on this success Space X was rewarded with a 1.6 billion dollar contract from NASA and Space X was on its way.

What can we learn from this? Once again, the road to success is NEVER a straight line. There will always be setbacks and disappointments when you try something new. You can count on it. One of Elon Musk's personal heroes was the great inventor Thomas Edison. Did you know that when Edison was attempting to invent a working light bulb he failed close to ten thousand times!?! Can you imagine how frustrating that must have been? It didn't bother Edison, however, as he knew with every failure he was getting closer to success!

"I have NOT failed. I've just found 10,000 ways that won't work." – Thomas Edison.

Throughout his life Elon Musk has followed Thomas Edison's example. When the first three Falcon 1 launches failed it would have been easy for Elon to have become discouraged. However, he never did. Like Edison, he kept his eye on the horizon, ignoring the choppy waves while continually moving towards his goal. Remember, you can never fail if you never give up!

Another lesson you can learn from Elon Musk and Space X is that if you want to accomplish something or make a change, then start small and build from there. Let's say you want to run a marathon, but you are not in very good shape. It would be crazy to try and run a marathon right off the bat! If you tried you'd be likely to pull a muscle or worse. Instead, the most important thing is to start small and build a habit. In this case you might start by waking up every morning and simply walking around the block. Once you get used to this you might try jogging around the block. As you get better you can jog for longer distances. Before you know it, you'll be ready to run that marathon!

Elon actually did the same thing with his rockets. His ultimate goal is to colonize Mars. Instead of building a gigantic rocket right off the bat though, he made the much smaller Falcon 1. From its success and failures, he learned enough to build the much more powerful Falcon 9. Once he got the Falcon 9 working well he used that to create the world's most powerful operational rocket, the Falcon Heavy. Just recently, he used the Falcon Heavy to launch one of his cars into space! I think you get the picture. Start small and build from there. It works for Elon Musk and it can work for you too.

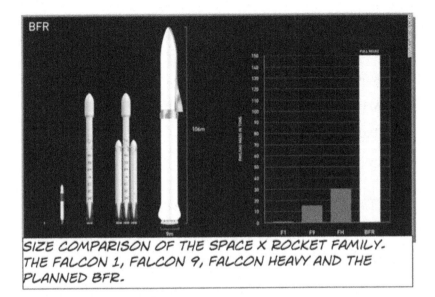

SIZE COMPARISON OF THE SPACE X ROCKET FAMILY. THE FALCON 1, FALCON 9, FALCON HEAVY AND THE PLANNED BFR.

So far, Space X has been an enormous success. Due to Elon's entrepreneurial ability he has reduced the cost of rockets reaching the International Space Station from 1 billion dollars to 60 million dollars! Very impressive, but Elon is not stopping there. He is currently having Tom and Space X design a new, reusable gigantic rocket called the BFR. (I'll let your parents explain what BFR likely stands for!) The BFR rockets are intended to replace the Falcon rocket family by 2020. Not only will they be able to perform all of the tasks that the Falcons could, but the BFR will also be powerful enough to reach Mars! Space X has made it a goal to launch a BFR to Mars in 2022 with a payload that will land on the red planet. For Elon Musk and Space X, the sky is NOT the limit, and neither is space itself!

"There's a fundamental difference, if you look into the future, between a humanity that is a space-faring civilization, that's out there exploring the stars ... compared with one where we are forever confined to Earth until some eventual extinction event" – Elon Musk discussing why he founded Space X.

Tesla

Elon Musk picks his projects and business opportunities by trying to find solutions to existing problems or projects that he thinks will benefit humanity. This is why he founded Space X. Elon has the dream of making humans an interplanetary species. Another problem that Elon saw was the issue of pollution. This is why he founded Tesla motors in 2003.

For Elon, the ultimate goal of Tesla is to create pollution free electric cars. He initially became interested in the electric car market when General Motors recalled its electric car, the EV1, in 2003. General Motors stopped making the EV1 because it didn't feel they could be made profitably. Elon thought that electric cars could be made profitably and that he was the one to do it!

TESLA MOTORS IS A WORLD LEADER IN ELECTRIC CAR DESIGN.

Elon's strategy for Tesla was very similar to how he built and improved his rockets for Space X. He started by making a high-end sports car. The sports car was very expensive and only a few were made. However, Tesla gained experience in making electric cars and will eventually be able to make cheaper, more consumer-friendly models.

The roadster that Tesla built was based on an existing car known as the Lotus Elise. In fact, the two cars are so similar that many people believe that the Tesla was merely an electric version of the Elise. This is in fact NOT true as the Tesla roadster only shares about 7% of its parts with the Elise. The Tesla Roadster sold for roughly $112,000, which was very expensive compared to similar gasoline cars in its class. For example, you could get a similar Mazda MX 5 for between $25,000 - $30,000. Nonetheless, over 2250 roadsters were sold worldwide and the people who bought them loved them. What is even more important is that the main goal of producing the roadster was accomplished. It proved that Tesla could produce an electric car and they gained tremendous knowledge in doing so.

Oh, and before we leave the Tesla Roadster here's some interesting trivia for you. Do you know who got the first Tesla Roadster when it came off the assembly line? None other than Elon Musk himself. This was also the car that he sent to Mars on top of the Heavy Falcon rocket. So, not only did Elon Musk own the first car that Tesla made, he also owned the first car to go into space!

ELON LAUNCHED HIS TESLA ROADSTER INTO SPACE!

Tesla next launched the Model S, a 5-door luxury liftback, on June 22, 2012. The car was well received and won many awards, including the Motor Trend Car of the Year and Automobile Magazine's Car of the Year. It also won the World Green Car of the year in 2013 and was the top selling plug-in electric car worldwide in 2015 and 2016.

A mid-sized, luxury crossover SUV, the Model X, was released by Tesla in September 2015. It was based on the Model S and shares about 60 percent of its content with its older sibling. The American Automobile Association named the

42

Model X its top green vehicle in 2017 and it ranked seventh in the world in terms of the best-selling plug-in cars in the world.

The most recent car that Tesla has released is the Model 3, which is a mid-sized four-door sedan. The base model can be purchased for $35,000, although more expensive upgrades are available. Nonetheless it represents the first car that Tesla has created that the average family could conceivably afford. This is demonstrated by the fact that Tesla had more than 325,000 reservations for the car within a week of it being announced, which is more than triple the amount the Model S had gotten in the same period of time.

By the end of 2017, Tesla had made the Fortune 500 (which is a list of the most valuable American companies compiled by Fortune magazine) and was one of the most valuable car companies in America. Does this mean it has been smooth sailing for Elon and Tesla? Once again, no. In the past, Tesla has repeatedly missed shipping dates and its cars have often cost more than originally promised. There have been manufacturing issues in which Tesla automobile plants have been unable to produce cars fast enough or of high enough quality. Although this is not ideal, it is not surprising. Elon is literally creating a new class of car from the ground up using new and unproven techniques. That there would be some hiccups and miscues along the way should not be surprising. Once again, though, Elon doesn't see "failure" or "mistakes" as being bad things. In fact, he revels in them as he sees in them opportunities to do things better and to improve. Every mistake literally helps Elon and Tesla produce better cars. As a result, I'm willing to bet that Elon and Tesla Motors are going to be around for a long time.

Solar City

The final Elon Musk company we will look at is Solar City. Solar City started as an idea Elon had to create a company that would build solar panels for home use. However, he was so busy with Tesla and Space X that he pitched the idea to two of his cousins, Lyndon and Peter Rive. That is how Solar City began with Lyndon and Peter Rive founding the company on the 4th of July, 2006.

The original business plan for Solar City was to offer their rooftop solar panels to potential customers by going door-to-door and offering solar leases. The idea behind leasing solar panels as opposed to buying them is similar to when people choose to lease a car. Essentially, you get the use of the car or, in this case, solar panels, without paying the full cost. With the incentives that many governments were offering at the time this meant that many Solar City customers were able to get solar panels installed for free, while Solar City collected all of the utility incentives and tax breaks. This "no-money-down solar" model proved to be very popular for Solar City, but it also proved to be very expensive. This resulted in Solar City growing very quickly, but it also added to Solar City's debt. If something wasn't done there was the possibility that Solar City could go out of business.

This is why Elon had Tesla buy Solar City in June 2016. Elon is committed to the idea of solar power and did not want to see Solar City die. He also thought that Tesla and Solar city could work well together with Tesla's battery complimenting Solar City's power products.

When Tesla took over Solar City the first thing they did was change its business model. It stopped offering leases as the company was losing too much money on them. From then on, if you wanted solar cells from Solar City, you were going to have to pay for them. Tesla also ended the practice of door-to-door sales. Door-to-door sales are expensive as you need to employ a lot of salespeople. However, for a new product like rooftop solar cells it had been effective. Despite this, Solar City had too much debt and cuts had to be made. The door-to-door sales force was one of them.

THE TESLA SOLAR ROOF, THE FUTURE OF SOLAR POWER.

At this point the future of Solar City is up in the air. However, the fact that it has a future at all is due to Elon Musk's commitment. In August 2016, Elon unveiled a new kind of solar cell called the Tesla Solar Roof. The idea behind the Solar Roof is to create roofing tiles that also function as solar cells. As Elon explains it, "It's not a thing on a roof. It is the roof." The response to the Tesla Solar Roof has been very positive and if Elon can bring it in at a reasonable price he may have a hit on his hands. Currently, the tiles are being manufactured at a Tesla factory in Buffalo, New

York (named the Gigafactory 2) and they should be made available to consumers in early 2018.

Life Lessons from Elon Musk

As you can see, Elon has had an extremely exciting and amazing life. What's more, he's not done yet. I'm just as excited, as you likely are too, to see what Elon comes up with in the future. I'm sure you're also interested in living a life full of achievement and possibility, just like Elon is. If so, what lessons can we take from his life and perhaps apply to our own? I've listed some below for you to consider, in no particular order.

Have a Vision in Life

If you are reading this and are young, then I know you will have a tough time believing this, but life goes by very fast. You are never too young to start taking the steps to become the young man or woman you want to become. For Elon, he decided he wanted to impact the world in the areas of the Internet, renewable energy and space exploration. How do you want to impact the world? Your goals need not be as lofty as Elon's. I mean, we can't have everyone founding companies like Space X! Despite that, it doesn't mean that you can't make an impact in your own way. The first step is to look after yourself. Clean your room and do not be a burden to others. From there you can start looking to help your family, friends, or community. You can do this in any number of ways. From volunteering somewhere to being the best you can be in whatever job you choose. What do you want to do? How can you help other people? Just decide and start doing it!

ELON WATCHING THE HEAVY FALCON LAUNCH.

Embrace Failure

You may be in school and you may think you are learning things there, and you are. However, let me assure you that you will only start to meet your real teachers, your life teachers, once you leave school. These teachers can be harsh and even cruel, but if you have the right attitude they can teach you lessons that will last a lifetime. The ultimate teacher you will meet, likely again and again, is failure. The important thing though is to not fear failure or attempt to skip his classes, but to embrace what he is teaching. As Elon says, failure is an essential part of the learning process because failure teaches us a great deal. Remember, the first 3 Falcon 1 rocket launches ended in failure, but Space X learned something from them each time. Never forget this when you make a mistake or when something goes wrong. Mistakes and failures are the ultimate teachers.

Embrace Criticism

This lesson is related to the last one, but in life it is important to embrace criticism. Once again, most people hate criticism, but constructive criticism can be extremely valuable as it helps you see things you might have missed. Elon actively seeks out constructive criticism whenever he can so that he can do and be better. Remember how Elon's friend tried to talk him out of building rockets? Elon took that criticism seriously. Although he ultimately went forward with Space X, he was under no delusions as to how hard it would be. This likely helped him work harder so that Space X would become a success.

"You should take the approach that you're wrong. Your goal is to be less wrong." – Elon Musk

Work Extremely Hard

If you're going to create something new and exciting, you'll have to work extremely hard. From his childhood Elon has always had an extremely strong work ethic. Likely this was partially developed by the chores that his father had Elon do. In Elon's way of thinking, you can accomplish the same thing in four months if you work one hundred hours a week vs. taking a year to do it and just working forty hours a week. Elon didn't get where he is by slacking. Oh, and do your chores, just like Elon did!

ELON DISCUSSING TESLA MOTOR CARS.

Never Stop Learning

Elon has always been a lifetime learner and is constantly learning something new. Jim Cantrell, the first vice president for business development at Space X, once suggested to Elon that he read a number of books on physics and rocketry. To his surprise, Elon read all of them in short order. This allowed him to talk to his engineers in their language and undoubtedly helped in the development of Space X's rockets.

Be Aware of Your Talent Stack and Work on Building It

Earlier, I mentioned the concept of the talent stack in relation to Elon Musk's achievements. For example, he was able to combine his entrepreneurial skills with his engineering know-how to create Space X. If he had only one of those skills, I'm sure he would have had great success in either of those occupations. However, by being able to combine both of them he was able to create an amazing company like Space X. Here's another great thing about talent stacks.

Even if you are only OK in certain areas, you can still combine your talents in unique ways.

I originally came across the concept of the "Talent Stack" in cartoonist Scott Adam's book "How to Fail at Almost Everything and Still Win Big" (a book I highly recommend, btw.) In it Scott describes his talent stack, which I've listed below:

He can draw, but he's not a great artist.

He can write, but he's never taken a writing class.

He's funny, but he knows others who are a lot funnier than he is.

He has business experience, but is in no way a great business mind.

From this list you can see that Scott has mediocre talents in four areas. There is nothing special there. However, when he combined them they allowed Scott to create the famous cartoon *Dilbert.*

THIS IS A GREAT BOOK ON LIFE STRATEGIES, INCLUDING THE TALENT STACK.

The key to the talent stack is that the talents in the stack work well together. If you acquire the right combination of ordinary talents you can achieve something unique. What talents do you have and how can they be combined? It's something to think about!

Dealing with Bullies

As you have learned, Elon Musk was bullied as a child. Why was he bullied? Likely because he was different from the other boys and was into doing his own things. No one should be bullied for this, yet it does happen. From my reading it appears that Elon didn't really take any steps to deal with his bullying. Below are some steps that he could have taken to handle that difficult situation better.

Actively Promote Confidence Through Body Language

Bullies are quick to pick up when people lack self-confidence. In the eyes of the potential bully this makes their potential victim that much more vulnerable. People who lack self-confidence project that feeling through their body language. They try to make themselves smaller than they are, they don't make eye contact, and they walk tentatively. Don't be like that. Even if you do not feel self-confident, pretend that you are. Stand up straight, walk with a purpose, and make eye contact with people. You may find this hard to believe until you experience it, but there is such a thing as a mind-body connection. When you walk with confidence, your mind will start to think that you *are* confident and before you know it you will start to feel that way. Mentally and physically, you will create a cycle of empowerment. Simply doing this can have the ability to stop any bullying before it starts.

Look to Actively Help Others

As a child Elon was obviously very smart, but he tended to keep to himself. Growing up is not easy. Do you think Elon would have had an easier time if he had been able to help other kids? Obviously, he was very good at school. Maybe he could have helped some of his classmates in areas they were having difficulty in. Here's the secret: when you help other people, they tend to want to help you too. Part of the reason Elon was bullied was because he was so isolated in school. If he had learned to help others in areas he was strong at, he would have likely been helped as well. People with friends are much less likely to be bullied. In any new school environment, try to help others whenever you can.

Do Not Be Afraid to Ask an Adult for Help
When Elon was being bullied he kept it to himself as much as he could and didn't tell anyone. Trying to avoid a problem in this way does not work. It didn't work for Elon and it will not work for you. Thankfully, people are much more aware of bullying today than they were in Elon's time. You should feel no shame in asking a teacher or a trusted adult for help. They are more than able to help. Always remember, you are not the first person to deal with issues like this and it's NOT your fault.

SUPERCHARGE YOUR BRAIN LIKE ELON WITH THIS EXERCISE.

This title is a little misleading, as it's impossible to think exactly like Elon Musk. Elon is obviously a unique individual, but, you know what? So are you! There has never been a person like you in the history of the world, and there never will be again. The key is to maximize your potential in every way possible. Below is a little mental training exercise that I think will help you do just that. It is to be done as soon as you wake up in the morning. You know how you probably feel groggy first thing in the morning and some people do some light stretches or exercises to wake their body up? This mental exercise is a form of brain training that will get your mind ready for maximum efficiency, just like Elon Musk. Here's what you do:

Perform this five-minute brain warm-up every morning before you get out of bed:

Count backwards from 100 to 0 as fast as you can.

Speed is key here so don't stop if you skip a number, just keep going!

Find a noun that fits each letter of the alphabet.

Don't just think of the word. Really imagine the shape, size, color and even smell of the object. Doing so will activate the left side of your brain (verbal, thinking of a word) and your right side (sizes, shapes, images, colors). This exercise will get both sides of your brain talking to each other and will therefore improve your mental performance. For example:

A – Android

B – Banana

C- Coconut

D – Dalmatian

etc.

Create a mental numbered list of female names, 1 – 10.

1 – Barbara

2 – Cheryl

3 – Julia

4 – Lydia

etc. until you get to 10.

Create a mental numbered list of male names, 1 – 10.

1 – Mark

2 – Steve

3 – Ben

4 – Brian

etc. until you get to 10.

Close your eyes and take 10 deep meditative breaths.

Breathe deeply through your nose and imagine that with each breath you are charging your brain. Imagine that the blood vessels and capillaries surrounding your brain are expanding and that your brain is crackling with thought energy.

That's it! Now open your eyes and start your day!

So, why does this brain exercise / warm-up work? It works because by performing these thought exercises you are forcing both hemispheres of your brain to work together. It improves your working memory because you have to keep track of just where you are in any given exercise. It teaches you how to think fast. It forces you to stretch your vocabulary. It forces you to get inside your head and focus.

I can't promise that this exercise will give you a brain like Elon Musk. I CAN promise, however, that this exercise will greatly increase your mental performance for the day. In this way, we can all be a little more like Elon Musk.

Elon Musk Quotes

"When something is important enough, you do it even if the odds are not in your favor."

"I think it's very important to have a feedback loop, where you're constantly thinking about what you've done and how you could be doing it better. I think that's the single best piece of advice: constantly think about how you could be doing things better and questioning yourself."

"If you get up in the morning and think the future is going to be better, it is a bright day. Otherwise, it's not."

ELON POSING IN FRONT OF THE SPACE X DRAGON CAPSULE.

"Patience is a virtue, and I'm learning patience. It's a tough lesson."

"It you're trying to create a company, it's like baking a cake. You have to have all the ingredients in the right proportion."

"I would like to die on Mars. Just not on impact."

"Some people don't like change, but you need to embrace change if the alternative is disaster."

"There's a silly notion that failure's not an option here. If things are not failing, you are not innovating enough."

"People should pursue what they're passionate about. That will make them happier than pretty much anything else."

"When Henry Ford made cheap, reliable care people said, 'Nah, what's wrong with a horse?' That was a huge bet he made, and it worked."

"I'm interested in things that change the world or that affect the future and wondrous, new technology where you see it, and you're like, 'Wow, how did that even happen? How is that possible?'"

"Any product that needs a manual to work is broken."

"Great companies are built on great products."

"People work better when they know what the goal is and why. It is important that people look forward to coming to work in the morning and enjoy working."

"When I was in college, I wanted to be involved in things that would change the world."

"I think it's the single best piece of advice: constantly think about how you could be doing things better and questioning yourself."

"There have to be reasons that you get up in the morning and you want to live. Why do you want to live? What's the point? What inspires you? What do you love about the future? If the future does not include being out there among the stars and being a multi-planet species, I find that incredibly depressing."

"It's OK to have your eggs in one basket as long as you control what happens to that basket."

"I don't create companies for the sake of creating companies, but to get things done."

"I had so many people try to talk me out of starting a rocket company, it was crazy."

"I think it matters whether someone has a good heart."

"Rockets are cool. There's no getting around that."

"Really, the only thing that makes sense is to strive for greater collective enlightenment."

"If you want to grow a giant redwood, you need to make sure the seeds are ok, nurture the sapling, and work out what might potentially stop it from growing all the way along. Anything that breaks it at any point stops that growth."

"I think we have a duty to maintain the light of consciousness to make sure it continues into the future."

"I think life on Earth must be about more than just solving problems... It's got to be something inspiring, even if it is vicarious."

"The odds of me coming into the rocket business, not knowing anything about rockets, not having every built anything, I mean, I would have to be insane if I thought the odds were in my favor."

"In order for us to have a future that's exciting and inspiring, it has to be one where we're a space-bearing civilization."

"America is the spirit of human exploration distilled."

"There are some important differences between me and Tony Stark, like I have five kids, so I spend more time going to Disneyland than parties."

Coming Soon!

At Biographies For Kids we are currently hard at work on our next book on the great Albert Einstein. More to come!

Check Out These Great Books Too!

We're big fans of Funny Comics, who make both educational and entertaining stories for kids. Below are some samples of their work. You can find all of their books and comics on Amazon!

Viva La Revolution!

In this fully illustrated comic time travelling friends Big Buddy and Little Buddy help George Washington!

Tear Down This Wall!

In this fully illustrated short story time travelling friends Big Buddy and Little Buddy help Ronald Reagan tear down the Berlin Wall!

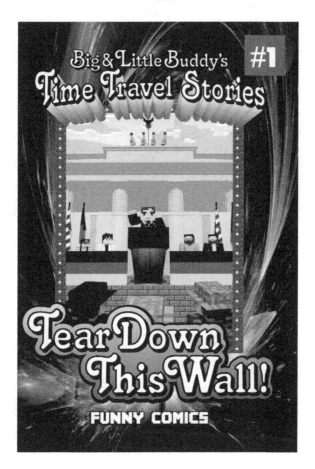

Jurassic Block

Funny Comics also has a series of parody comics based on famous movies like Jurassic Park, Star Wars and The Avengers.

What Should Our Next Biography Be?

The biography you have currently read is on the great Elon Musk. The next book we are working on is Albert Einstein. Who should we write about next? If you have any ideas, let us know! To do this, please consider leaving a review for THIS book on Amazon and let us know whom you would like to see be the focus of our next book. The review would really help us out and will help us learn who you are interested in reading about. So, let us know! Lily says thank-you in advance for helping us!